Copyright © 2024 Jessica Hottle

All rights reserved, including the right to reproduce this book or portions of this book in any form whatsoever without the prior written permission of the copyright holder.

Scripture quotations marked esv are taken from the ESV® Bible (The Holy Bible, English Standard Version®), copyright © 2001 by Crossway, a publishing ministry of Good News Publishers. Used by permission. All rights reserved.

Scripture quotations marked tlb are taken from The Living Bible copyright© 1971. Used by permission of Tyndale House Publishers, Inc., Carol Stream, Illinois 60188. All rights reserved.

Limits of Liability and Disclaimer of Warranty
The author and publisher shall not be liable for your misuse of this material. This book is strictly for informational and educational purposes.

The purpose of this book is to educate and entertain. The author and/or publisher does not guarantee that anyone following these techniques, suggestions, tips, ideas, or strategies will become successful. The author and/or publisher shall have neither liability nor responsibility to anyone with respect to any loss or damage caused, or alleged to be caused, directly or indirectly by the information contained in this book.

Cover design and layout by Allison Capps.

Stress and Anxiety

BIBLICAL STUDY

Jessica Hottle

Introduction

    The body is constantly communicating, telling you something. Tense muscles, rapid heartbeat, shallow breathing, sweating, and constant fidgeting are a few signs and ways our bodies are telling us it's perceiving a threat. When our bodies perceive a threat or stress of any kind that can trigger our anxious feelings, what happens next is our bodies' fight-or-flight response kicks in and begins to take care of us according to the information it is receiving. In other words, our bodies are trying to get our attention and tell us something. Will we listen?

    With the fast pace of this world, it's no wonder we are finding ourselves in a constant state of anxious feelings. We feel there is no time to slow down and appropriately respond to the situations and things happening to us and around us. We think to ourselves we will deal with it later until later never comes, and we find ourselves lying awake at night trying to process everything all at once. A time when everything seems to sink in without noise or distractions. A time we usually want to escape from - silence with our own thoughts. It's no wonder we have an anxiety epidemic.

    You are not alone. In 2022 and 2023, an average of 37.1% of women and 29.9% of men reported high levels of anxiety. Compared to data from 2012 to 2015, this has increased significantly from 21.8% of women and 18.3% of men reporting high levels of anxiety (Mental Health Foundation, 2023). According to the ADAA, "women are twice as likely to be affected as men" (ADAA, 2023). This epidemic is affecting Americans at an astounding rate, but the good news is that the Bible offers wisdom and encouragement in dealing with these feelings. Bringing comfort to our weariness and strength through Him when we feel the heaviness in our chest, His word is available to help us.

Anxiety is usually our reaction to stress, something we are dealing with internally. We will work together in this study to identify the differences and similarities between stress and anxiety. Using this study, you can identify those stressors by asking questions to help you process what is causing you stress so you can partner with God in finding solutions and rest in His healing.

Together, we will explore how biblical teachings can bring comfort and hope when facing the challenges of stress and anxiety. This biblical study will help guide you through anxiety, renew your thoughts, and lead you to the cross for healing. God acknowledges our human struggles (our humanity), including our everyday stressors that produce anxiety within us. Hebrews 4:15-16 reminds us that we can go to Him boldly with our struggles,

For we do not have a high priest who is unable to sympathize with our weaknesses, but one who in every respect has been tempted as we are, yet without sin. 16 Let us then with confidence draw near to the throne of grace, that we may receive mercy and find grace to help in time of need.

You may be someone who struggles with anxiety right now and has anxious feelings, but that is not your identity. Nothing you feel or are going through impacts how God loves you or how much He loves you. Your worth isn't placed in your strengths or your weaknesses. You have value because you were made in the image of your Father. There is nothing that can change that. God defines who you are; your identity is not based on any description of your current circumstances or struggles.

Please Note: *This book is for informational purposes only and seeks to address stress and anxiety concerns from a clinically-informed and biblically grounded perspective. This resource is not intended to substitute for professional advice, diagnosis, or treatment. To be diagnosed or treated for anxiety, anxiety disorders, stress-related mental health challenges, or any other physical or mental health concerns, please seek out your trusted medical provider. This is not a resource for emergency or crisis help.*

Defining Stress and Its Impact

Every day, when our alarms go off and our eyes open, we begin making decisions. By the end of the day, when our heads hit the pillow to do it all over again, we would have made an estimated 35,000 decisions (Graff, 2021). I don't know about you, but that feels like a lot to me. Between taking care of the family, what to eat, work situations, friendships, processing the pain we carry, and reading our Bibles (to name a few), it can all feel like too much at times. But we have to do it, right? The family needs to be fed, we need to go to work, and our friendships are important, so the question becomes how do we steward what God has entrusted to us without living overwhelmed by stress or filled with anxiety day in and day out.

Let's first start this process by defining stress. According to mentalhealth.org, "Stress is the feeling of being overwhelmed or unable to cope with mental or emotional pressure." According to Don Colbert, M.D., "stress is mental or physical tension, strain or pressure" (Colbert, D. 2020, p.8). However, stress researchers and authors Doc Childre and Howard Martin say, "Stress is the body and mind's response to any pressure that disrupts their normal balance. It occurs when our perceptions of events don't meet our expectations, and we don't manage our reaction to the disappointment." (Colbert, D. 2020, p.8-9) Therefore, stress comes in many different forms, and our perceptions are the difference between how we all deal with stress. When a decision in our day disrupts our normal balance or causes strain and pressure, how we view that particular situation will shape the level of stress we put ourselves under.

In order to address stress, we need to understand it. The three parts of stress are the event itself, our perception of it, and how we manage it. What stresses me may not stress you. What worries me may not worry you. Why? Because we both perceive events and situations differently, stress is subjective.

For example, let's think of stress as a daily commute. For one person, it might be frustrating with traffic jams, delays, and constant roadblocks. This individual may start to feel overwhelmed, irritated, drained by the end of the commute, and frustrated by the time they get to their destination.

On the other hand, someone else might view the same commute as an opportunity for personal growth and prayer. They use the time to listen to educational podcasts, practice mindfulness, listen to the audio version of the Bible, or enjoy audiobooks. This person sees the commute as a chance to learn and develop new skills amidst roadblocks and travel delays.

In this example, stress is the commute, and the varying perspectives represent how our views shape the impact of stress. The way we approach and interpret the challenges can either make it a draining experience or an opportunity for personal development. The beautiful thing about God's love is that it requires choice. Therefore, as we go about our day, knowing we have free will, we will have to decide what perspective we will choose: God's desires and way or our way. I know from experience that our way often leads to burnout and exhaustion.

Two Types of Stress

Stress falls into two types: controllable and uncontrollable. Controllable stress is related to situations or factors over which we have some influence or control. For example, deadlines at work, managing time, and setting priorities are aspects of life where individuals can take action and make decisions to reduce stress. In controllable stress, there is a sense of empowerment to change or improve the circumstances.

Uncontrollable stress, on the other hand, involves situations or factors that are beyond our control. Events like natural disasters, the actions of others, or unexpected health issues fall into this category. In uncontrollable stress, individuals may feel a lack of power to alter the situation, leading to a higher level of emotional strain.

Understanding this distinction is crucial because it affects how we cope with stress. Proactive measures and problem-solving strategies can be applied to controllable stress. In contrast, managing uncontrollable stress takes us to a deeper level of trust in the Father, accepting things we can not control, and coping mechanisms to navigate challenging circumstances that cannot be changed.

Stress is not specifically mentioned in the Bible. However, worry, troubles, and anxiety are. Which are merely a symptom of stress, and stress is a symptom of our perception. Think of a symptom as the fruit of whatever has roots in your heart. In my book, Face Off with Your Feelings, I have a whole section on how to uproot worry and the lies to create new fruit. This process utilizes truths from God's Word to aid the process.

Pain a Source of Stress

When we think about stress, we can also think about how our pain has altered our view of the world. Pain can come from two different sources – a violation of love, which tells us who we are, and a violation of trust, which makes us feel unsafe. So we might feel helpless and powerless, or we might feel like we're unable to measure up to expectations, that we're inadequate, or that we're not good enough for the task we're being asked to do.

Therefore, our perception of what is happening around us can also lead to worry. What I see the most often with worry is that our brain starts trying to help us out by controlling more than we're able to by overthinking it and worrying about it. And usually, that's a sign that we've stepped beyond what we're empowered to do, beyond what we have agency over and choices in. We're starting to worry about it because we're in territory that we don't have any control over.

A major component when we feel unsafe or when we feel helpless or powerless is being able to say, "Okay, I may not be able to control the entirety of this situation; I may not even be able to control very much of it, but I am a human being who is empowered by God to make wise choices." We can narrate this situation for ourselves. We want to be aware of our choices, what we would love to control, and what we can't. Doing this helps us recognize God's part and our part.

Psalm 46:1-3 paints a beautiful picture of how God is with us and strengthening us,

> *God is our refuge and strength, a very present help in trouble. <u>Therefore</u> we will not fear though the earth gives way, though the mountains be moved into the heart of the sea, though its waters roar and foam, though the mountains tremble at its swelling.*

In His kindness, He isn't only our refuge but also our strength. That means He not only shelters us from and in times of trouble but also gives us strength to overcome. His help is not only defensive but offensive too. His presence with us is foundational to feeling safe and gives us the strength and courage to live each day.

Journal Exercise:

    A great journal exercise that I will have clients work through for worries and stress about a situation is to draw two large circles on a piece of paper and brainstorm their choices. Label the first circle "Control." In the first circle, answer the following question: What are all the things I can control and am able to put my energy toward that actually make a difference? Label the second circle "Surrender." In the second circle, list all the things you would love to be able to control but can't. If you are someone who loves Jesus, then I think it's a great prayer exercise to prayerfully hand that other circle over, knowing that you can trust God with all the things you have no agency over. Surrender to God what's His to worry about and take action on the things listed in the "Control" Circle.

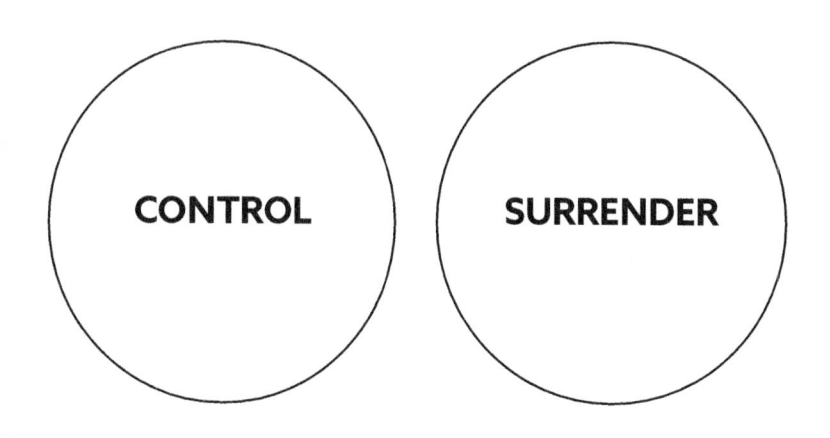

CONTROL   **SURRENDER**

Everyday Stressors and Their Impact

Now that we have a better understanding of what stress is and how God is with us, strengthening us, we can take a look at what kinds of stressors we experience in our lives and begin to take inventory. Our bodies don't care or know what caused the stress. All our bodies know is that they are experiencing stress.

Sources of Stress

1. Accelerated pace of life: think about how Jesus walked everywhere; he was never in a hurry and never ran.
2. Intensified level of arousal: the digital world, smartphones.
3. Increased rate of change: faster than ever, instant gratification.
4. More complex social settings and interactions: the internet complicates it more, loss of face-to-face interaction.
5. Inadequate time for recovery: we now sleep less than ever before

When our pace of life increases, our time spent scrolling is higher than ever, and we are striving to make it by ourselves; with little to no sleep, our body begins to kick into overdrive. The stress response (fight or flight) fights for us on our behalf to keep us alive and functioning.

When our stress response never gets a break (when the perceived threat is always a threat), a few things begin to happen in our bodies with time:

1. Increase in pain (reduced endorphins)
2. Increased anxiety (reduced natural tranquilizers)
3. Increased cardiovascular disease
4. Reduced immune system
5. Increased fatigue and possible depression (reduced adrenaline resources)
6. Psychological disruption of life (American Psychological Association, 2023).

Eventually, when we ignore the signs and cues our bodies give us, what was once manageable, situational stress (increased productivity, energy, etc.) gives rise to distress. Unresolved distress can cause anxiety, high blood pressure, and increased cholesterol, which could turn into stress disease (enlarged adrenals, narrowing of the arteries, sleep disorders) (the Advisory Committee on Colleague Assistance, 2008). Chronic stress has lasting consequences on the body.

When stress sticks around for too long, it messes with how your body works. Your body produces cortisol, a natural stress manager, but if stress sticks around, it can tire out the part that makes cortisol—the adrenal glands. This tiredness can throw off important functions. Your immune system, the defender against sickness, may not work as well, making you more prone to getting sick. Your metabolism, which controls weight and sugar levels, can act up, causing weight gain and issues with sugar levels. Sleep might become a challenge, making it harder to get good rest. Your memory and focus might also be affected, and there's a higher risk of facing long-term health problems like heart issues and diabetes.

Stress Self-Check

Utilize the following self-check-in to evaluate your own stress levels. Choose the word or words that best describe your situation. Please discuss your observations with a counselor, therapist, or care provider.

- My daily pace of life feels... frantic... sustainable... too slow...
- My weekly pace of life feels... frantic... sustainable... too slow...
- As I go throughout my day, I feel... stressed... calm... exhausted...
- At the end of the day, I feel... fulfilled... overstimulated... stressed...
- My quality of sleep is... poor... good... excellent...
- When I need to wait, I feel... irritated... bored... calm...
- My relationships feel... satisfying... dull... fulfilling...
- My community feels like it's... engaged... developing... disconnected...
- My down time feels... depleting... neutral... energizing...
- My physical energy level feels... unpredictable... depleted... renewable...
- My pain level most often feels... high... medium... low...
- My anxiety level most often feels... high... medium... low...
- My heart rate most often feels... high... medium... low...
- I find myself feeling/ getting sick... often... occasionally... rarely if ever...
- I wake up feeling tired... often... occasionally... rarely if ever...

Through the stresses of life and the wearing out of our bodies, Paul gives us hope in 2 Corinthians 4:7-12,

> *But we have this treasure in jars of clay, to show that the surpassing power belongs to God and not to us. We are afflicted in every way, but not crushed; perplexed, but not driven to despair; persecuted, but not forsaken; struck down, but not destroyed; always carrying in the body the death of Jesus, so that the life of Jesus may also be manifested in our bodies. For we who live are always being given over to death for Jesus' sake, so that the life of Jesus also may be manifested in our mortal flesh. So death is at work in us, but life in you.*

Let's go a little deeper into what Paul is saying here. Paul shares what we will experience living in this world: affliction, a state of being perplexed, persecuted, and struck down.

- The Greek word for "afflicted" is used to convey a sense of being in a state of distress, suffering, or hardship. It is often associated with experiencing trouble, affliction, or adversity (Bible Hub, 2024).
- The Greek word for "perplexed" is derived from the root "Άπορος" (aporos), which means "without resources" or "in difficulty." In the context of being perplexed, it implies a state of confusion, uncertainty, or being at a loss for a solution or direction (Bible Hub, 2024).

- The Greek word for "persecution" is used to describe the act of persecuting, harassing, or pursuing someone with hostility (Bible Hub, 2024).
- The Greek phrase "cast down" is often used metaphorically to express a state of being brought low, humbled, or cast down in spirit (Bible Hub, 2024).

Paul wanted us to know the world, our flesh, and sin is going to try and take us out, but it doesn't have to keep us down. We will have hardships and suffer. There are times when we will be confused and uncertain. In our walk with God, we will have people degrade, judge, and harass us based on what we believe. Through all of that, it can be easy for us to be brought low. No matter what we feel, Paul reminds us that God is with us, and with His strength, we will not be crushed, driven to despair, forsaken, or destroyed. Our perspective, where we set our gaze, is how we continue to show up when we want to shut down. When we look at Jesus, He carries the weight of what we feel.

Paul continues in verse 16 to say,

So we do not lose heart. Though our outer self is wasting away, our inner self is being renewed day by day. For this light momentary affliction is preparing for us an eternal weight of glory beyond all comparison, as we look not to the things that are seen but to the things that are unseen. For the things that are seen are transient, but the things that are unseen are eternal.

Paul ends this chapter with hope and a reminder: Our outer man (our physical bodies are decaying), but our inner strength is renewing day by day because of Jesus at work within us. Do not grow weary (do not lose heart) when the weight of the stress and situations feel unbearable. We were never meant to carry that weight by ourselves. We find rest for our souls when our hearts are calibrated toward His. God is Jehovah-Rapha, the Healer of our souls.

The Stress Response

Now that we have defined stress, what causes stress, and its impact, let's talk about how fight-or-flight is our body's response to survival. Our sympathetic nervous system is what drives the fight-or-flight or the stress response. Its response is to stimulate cortisol and adrenaline to mobilize us to fight or flee from danger. The amygdala interprets the images and sounds and then sends a signal to the hypothalamus. The hypothalamus then communicates to the rest of the body, through the nervous system, how it needs to respond. We can view the hypothalamus as a command center (Harvard Medical School, 2020).

When we are constantly stressed and talking about how stressed we are, our bodies never leave a state of fight-or-flight. Our body protects us at all costs and is preparing for battle. Suppose our brains continue to view situations as dangerous. In that case, our brains will continue to send signals to our bodies, traveling to the pituitary glands, which release hormones that trigger the adrenals to produce cortisol.

Sometimes, the smallest things can trigger emotions that fill us with regret. White-knuckling is an example of how we might try to push (and rush) through the day, experiences, and our everyday life. If we were in a game of tug-of-war, we would have our hands wrapped around the rope so tightly because we do not want to lose. In our attempt to win, we grip so hard that our knuckles become white, and the rope beneath our palms burns our hands. We may white-knuckle our lives consciously or unconsciously, but we ignore the warning signs from our brains and our bodies that God designed specifically to help us cope. A few examples of this are ignoring hunger pains, apologizing for our feelings, and minimizing our feelings as not being so bad—or maybe a Netflix binge or picking up our phone more than a hundred times a day to distract ourselves.

Understanding fight-or-flight at its most basic level is essential to understand why we show up the way we do in certain situations. Learning how our body responds gives us the ability to pull away and into healing. God didn't create us to live this life by "just getting by." He came for us so we may have an abundant life. Even with the stress of this world, "God gave us a spirit not of fear but of power and love and self-control" (2 Timothy 1:7). Living in past experiences and emotions as if they are happening now can directly impact our health.

These experiences and our beliefs about them can impact how we live in the present and our future reality. There might be times when we do not realize when this is happening. Still, we may begin to notice an increase in heart rate and blood pressure, or we may begin to feel anxious.

We are spirits with a tender soul at home within a physical body where all parts communicate together. Our past is no mystery to God, but our past can guide us through our present responses. The more we look at our past to learn about our present, the better we can equip ourselves.

Our present response has a lot to do with how our past experiences have trained our parasympathetic and sympathetic nervous systems—parts of our physical bodies. The sympathetic nervous system controls our fight-or-flight response. Our sympathetic nervous system acts like a green light that says, "All systems are ready to go and respond." The sympathetic nervous system triggers our fight or flight response, which tells our body how to respond to the current situation we are dealing with.

The nervous system is sizing up the threat. Should we run? Do we stay and fight? Is now the time to shut down and draw away? Understanding our fight-or-flight response allows us to begin to have compassion for ourselves and those around us.

When we live in fight-or-flight mode, we cannot connect to the areas of our bodies that give us the ability to solve problems and reason. I spent most of my life relying on the same fight-or-flight response method of coping that I always had: defense based on fear. I knew only how to survive instead of live. It actually felt like my body was at war with my mind and soul. My soul wanted something different, something more than survival. However, my body was just going through all the motions because life demanded that things get done. My soul was screaming for my body to slow down and allow it to catch up with my body. God designed our bodies to tell the stories of our souls. The question is, will we listen?

Deep Breathing Exercise:
Engaging in deep breathing exercises is an effective way to calm the nervous system and shift it out of the "fight or flight" mode. Here's a simple deep belly breathing exercise:

1. Find a Quiet Space: Sit or lie down in a comfortable position in a quiet space.
2. Place Your Hand on Your Belly: Put one hand on your chest and the other on your belly.
3. Inhale Slowly: Breathe in slowly through your nose, letting your belly rise. Focus on filling your lungs with air.
4. Exhale Gradually: Breathe out slowly through your mouth or nose, letting your belly fall. Imagine releasing tension with each exhale.
5. Repeat: Continue this deep breathing for several breaths, making each inhale and exhale deliberate and calming.

This exercise activates the body's relaxation response, helping to reduce stress hormones and promote a sense of calm. It's a simple yet powerful way to shift your nervous system from "fight or flight" to a more relaxed state.

Stress versus Anxiety

What is the difference between stress and anxiety? How do we know if it's just stress we are dealing with or anxiety? Let's look at it this way. Imagine stress and anxiety as unwelcome guests in your house. Stress is like a temporary visitor who knocks on your door, bringing extra responsibilities or challenges. It might make you a bit busy or overwhelmed, but eventually, it leaves when the situation gets better.

On the other hand, anxiety is more like a persistent guest who overstays their welcome. It's as if anxiety has settled in, making you feel uneasy and on edge even when there's no immediate threat. While stress is a response to external pressures, anxiety tends to linger internally, creating a sense of worry and fear that can stick around longer than you'd like.

In this analogy, stress is a short-term guest, and anxiety is a more persistent, long-term visitor that requires extra attention and care to manage and eventually ease out of your "house" or life. Therefore, stress is a response to an external cause, such as arguing with a friend or work deadlines. It will go away once the situation is resolved. Stress can be positive or negative, encouraging us to meet a deadline or causing us to lose sleep. However, anxiety is generally internal, meaning it's our reaction to stress (National Institute of Mental Health). The feelings never seem to go away; they linger even when the situation is resolved. Both can affect our bodies the same way, though. We may experience worry, headaches, loss of sleep, or low energy.

Why does all of this matter? When we misdiagnose, we mistreat. When we understand what we are going through, we can find proper solutions to help us through those times. As we learn, we understand that we should no longer take automatic thoughts that come our way at face value. We can learn how to dissect, examine, and question our thoughts. Examining our thoughts can help develop a habit of questioning any negative beliefs, assumptions, or projections. What we feel isn't always the truth. What we feel isn't who we are and doesn't make us "unusable" by God. We must know what we are dealing with before we try to solve the problem.

We can find comfort in knowing God partnered with people who faced intense amounts of stress and or worry at different times in their lives. They were not less (or greater) than anyone else, but the difference was their trust was not in what they were feeling. Oftentimes, they didn't understand and were crying out to God, physically feeling the pain, but their heart knew God was not giving this to them but that God was with them. I want to share a few people who didn't live perfect lives or were without struggles but individuals who, within the struggle, were honest, vulnerable, and sought after God's heart.

Job endured immense suffering, losing his wealth, health, and family. His story is a testament to perseverance and faith in the face of profound adversity. In the Book of Job, there are numerous instances where Job expresses his distress and anguish, particularly in the form of lamentations. One specific example is found in Job 3:1-26. After experiencing immense suffering, including the loss of his wealth, health, and family, Job begins to lament his existence, expressing the depth of his despair. In Job 3:20-23, Job says,

> *Why is light given to him who is in misery, and life to the bitter in soul, who long for death, but it comes not, and dig for it more than for hidden treasures, who rejoice exceedingly and are glad when they find the grave? Why is light given to a man whose way is hidden, whom God has hedged in?*

In these verses, Job shares his anguish and the desire for death as a relief from his suffering. This passage reflects the depth of Job's emotional distress during a particularly challenging time in his life and teaches us to lament and cry out in our own suffering.

     David faced numerous challenges, including threats to his life, betrayal, and guilt for his mistakes. The Psalms, attributed to David, often express his raw emotions and struggles. One specific instance where David expressed stress can be found in the Psalms. In Psalm 55:4-5 David shares his feelings of distress and anxiety, *"My heart is in anguish within me; the terrors of death have fallen upon me. Fear and trembling come upon me, and horror overwhelms me."* In these verses, David openly expresses his inner turmoil, describing feelings of anguish, fear, and overwhelming horror. This psalm reflects a moment of deep emotional stress and the challenges David faced, providing a glimpse into his humanity as well as his reliance on God during times of trouble.

Elijah, a prophet, experienced moments of intense stress, especially when he faced opposition from Queen Jezebel and sought refuge in the wilderness, expressing feelings of despair even to the point of asking God to take his life. Elijah's plea is expressed in 1 Kings 19:4,

> *But he himself went a day's journey into the wilderness and came and sat down under a broom tree. And he asked that he might die, saying, 'It is enough; now, O Lord, take away my life, for I am no better than my fathers.'*

Elijah's plea reflects the depth of his distress and weariness in the face of his challenges and threats. This time in Elijah's life highlights the reality of emotional struggles, even in the lives of strong and faithful people.

Jeremiah, known as the "weeping prophet," faced opposition, rejection, and the challenging task of delivering messages of judgment. His ministry was marked by personal distress. One specific instance is found in Jeremiah 20:14-18, where Jeremiah laments his existence and the challenges he faces in delivering God's messages,

> *Cursed be the day on which I was born! The day when my mother bore me, let it not be blessed! Cursed be the man who brought the news to my father, 'A son is born to you,' making him very glad. Let that man be like the cities that the Lord overthrew without pity; let him hear a cry in the morning and an alarm at noon, because he did not kill me in the womb; so my mother would have been my grave, and her womb forever great.*

In these verses, Jeremiah expresses a deep sense of despair and curses the day of his birth due to the hardships he faces in delivering God's messages. This passage illustrates the emotional toll and personal struggles of a prophet called to proclaim challenging messages to the people. Jeremiah's experience reflects the complex relationship between the prophet and the difficult task set before him.

The apostle Paul faced various hardships, including persecution, imprisonment, and physical ailments. In his letters, he openly shared the pressures he encountered in spreading the message of Christ. In 2 Corinthians 1:8-9, Paul writes,

> *For we do not want you to be unaware, brothers, of the affliction we experienced in Asia. For we were so utterly burdened beyond our strength that we despaired of life itself. Indeed, we felt that we had received the sentence of death. But that was to make us rely not on ourselves but on God who raises the dead.*

In these verses, Paul openly shares his intense challenges, feeling burdened beyond his strength to despairing in life. This moment of stress and hardship becomes a testament to Paul's reliance on God and the understanding that his reliance on divine strength is crucial. The apostle's experiences, as recorded in his letters, reveal the human side of his faith journey and the trials he encountered in spreading the message of Christ.

Jesus, in the Garden of Gethsemane, experienced profound stress and anguish before His crucifixion. He prayed fervently, grappling with the weight of His impending sacrifice. The account of Jesus sweating blood is found in the Gospel of Luke 22:44, *"And being in agony, he prayed more earnestly; and his sweat became like great drops of blood falling down to the ground."* This moment occurred in the Garden of Gethsemane, just before Jesus' arrest and crucifixion. The intensity of Jesus' prayer and the distress he experienced is vividly described, symbolized by the rare and profound phenomenon of sweating blood. It reflects the immense weight and anticipation of the sacrifice he was about to make for humanity's redemption. This event is a powerful depiction of Jesus' humanity, his willingness to fulfill His purpose, and the depth of his pain.

      Each of these stories resonates with our shared humanity, reminding us that it's natural to feel the weight of life's challenges. Yet, within these struggles, there is an enduring message of hope—that we can find strength through faith, resilience, and reliance on God in our weakness. Just as Job, David, Elijah, Jeremiah, and Paul found peace in their trials, so too can we. As we do, we can begin to normalize having conversations around suffering without it becoming a normal way of living. We don't need to hide from God or pretend everything is fine when it's not. Living a holy life isn't defined by our feelings, denying our feelings, or pretending our pain doesn't exist. We can have comfort knowing we are in good company with others who have suffered before us.

Defining Anxiety

As we think about the challenges faced by people in the Bible, it's clear that stress is something everyone deals with. Today, we often find ourselves grappling with anxiety, which is a close companion to stress. Like people in the Bible felt stress, we, too, feel the weight of anxiety in our lives. Yet, just as they discovered strength and hope in their struggles, we can learn from their experiences and find ways to navigate the complexities of anxiety in our own lives. Let's take a closer look now at anxiety. What is it, and how does it impact our lives?

Anxiety is a response to stress (Ross, 2018). I like to consider anxiety a secondary emotion. Another word for that might be more of a reaction than a feeling or a primary emotion. Anxiety is like a backup emotion that shows up when we feel other strong emotions like fear, sadness, or anger. Imagine it as a warning signal telling us there might be something challenging ahead. It's our mind getting ready to deal with tough situations or uncertainties. So, anxiety is like a response to those first feelings, helping us get ready to handle whatever comes our way.

Anxiety acts as a protective mechanism, alerting us to potential threats and preparing us to cope with or avoid adverse outcomes. It can be seen as a natural response that helps mobilize cognitive and physiological resources to deal with stressors. Understanding anxiety as a secondary emotion highlights its connection to underlying feelings and the intricate ways our emotional responses unfold. In short, anxiety is your body's reaction to stress and can occur even if there is no current threat.

Some people suggest that anxiety is cognitive dissonance (when your beliefs don't line up with your actions) created by a divided mind (Suinn, 1965). Holding two beliefs creates tension because they do not agree with each other. If we feel anxious, it could be that somewhere inside ourselves, we are arguing with ourselves. Paul tells us in Philippians 4:6, "Do not be anxious about anything, but in everything by prayer and supplication with thanksgiving let your requests be made known to God." The Greek meaning for anxious in this verse is "divided into parts" or to be divided (A. T. Robertson); (figuratively) "to go to pieces" because pulled apart (in different directions), like the force exerted by sinful anxiety (worry) (Bible Hub, 2024). First, a personal example: I started to feel anxious when life's stressors seemed to pile up too fast, especially the moments I didn't see coming. The feelings continue when I feel like I have to constantly choose and make a decision while feeling this internal battle of beliefs. Another example is one of my coaching clients who described to me one day how she felt a lot of anxious feelings while at work, knowing what she should be doing but not being able to be productive. There is something happening within the mind, dividing our thoughts, attention, and focus when anxiety is at play.

No matter how we experience them, anxious feelings are indicators of something deeper happening with our minds and bodies. God created our bodies with an incredible ability to handle stress, kind of like a built-in survival kit. This shows us that God made us strong and adaptable, ready to face whatever comes our way.

Exercise: Journal through these questions. Ask the Holy Spirit to guide you and bring anything you can't see about your anxiety or stress into the light so the darkness can no longer overpower them.

1. How would you describe your anxious feelings?

2. When do your anxious feelings come?

3. What thoughts are you toggling between?

4. Do you find yourself having an internal battle or struggle where your thoughts compete and fight against each other?

5. How do you typically handle anxious feelings when you have them?

6. What is one thing you can implement that you know would help with your anxious feelings?

7. When will you start implementing it, and how?

Anxiety in Your Body

In order to care well for our bodies, we need to work to recognize normal stressors from anxious feelings. With anxiety, feelings of persistent dread and worry are present even when the threat is gone. There's not something to fear, but we interpret it that way. Therefore, our bodies activate, and this activation takes place in the brain. When anxiety is present, and we are interpreting a threat that may not be real, the part of your brain that is responsible for reasoning, decision-making, planning, and sound judgment shuts down. When we're triggered (our bodies believe there is a threat), is when our brain sends signals to our amygdala, the fear center of the brain, quicker than it goes to the frontal lobes – the thinking and planning center. We can even begin to feel it physically with fatigue, tight shoulders, and headaches. While these things are common, this should not be our normal way of living.

This process the brain goes through is called "amygdala hijacking" (Guy-Evans, 2023). Think of your brain as a control center; the amygdala is like a tiny security guard on duty. Its job is to keep an eye out for threats. Now, when it senses danger, it can react really fast – even before the thinking part of our brain kicks in. That's what we call an "amygdala hijack"! It's like the security guard hitting the emergency button without checking with the boss. In real life, this happens when something scares or stresses us, and we react before our thinking brain gets a chance to catch up. Understanding that this is naturally the way the brain functions helps us manage our reactions better, giving the thinking part of our brain a chance to respond more calmly.

Likely, all of us have experienced when anxiety takes over so significantly that we lose the ability to reason in our minds. We may even feel a little stuck. We become unable to see our way out of the situation. In this scenario, the fear response is literally hijacking the brain. Everything experienced happens to our entire being. It impacts our brain and our organs, skin, and physical body. For example, I coach and counsel women to help them manage the mental stresses of life through the working of God's love. However, a lot of the women I work with are trying to do everything they can outwardly, such as reading more or praying more. Yet, they don't realize that the denial of their feelings and poor stewardship with pushing their bodies to perform through fear is also impacting how they manage their mental stress.

This is why we can not simply throw scriptures at ourselves about stress and anxiety and hope it all goes away. The event, situation, or trauma happened to all of you emotionally, spiritually, and physically. God's transformation works from the inside out, not the outside in. He works from the spiritual to the natural. Jesus tells us to abide in the vine, to renew our minds, and to train ourselves in godliness. We use our whole bodies to find wholeness with Him.

Practical Techniques to Help with Anxiety

Now that we have an understanding of the differences between anxiety and stress and how the body tells the soul story, we need practical tools and techniques to help us process and manage these emotions. Time heals all wounds is a common phrase, but that is actually a lie. Time can soften the intensity and frequency of these intense feelings, but time doesn't make what we feel disappear. Feelings do not just dissipate. Stress and anxiety do not vanish. They transform into something better (like anger can transform into forgiveness) or bigger (like anger becoming rage), depending on how we feed into them. The goal of collecting and learning to use tools is to create space between us and the emotion to focus our souls on God's truth.

I John 3:20 serves as a reminder that God is greater than our feelings and knows every detail about our hearts: "For if our heart condemns us, God is greater than our heart, and knows all things." We can't run from Him, and He never hides from us. Knowing He is greater brings us comfort and spiritual safety because He is our source of truth, not what we feel. When we know God never leaves us, even in our turmoil, we realize that time will not fix what we are going through; we must pursue healing. We can engage with the Lord and find safety in Him and His word as we learn and use the tools we need for anxiety and stress.

The first technique for overcoming stress and anxiety is attentional control. Attentional control is our ability to concentrate or to choose what we pay attention to. This may be limited at first but can grow with practice over time.

For those of us grappling with intense anxiety that makes it challenging to maintain focus, I recommend taking small, practical steps. Start with simple mindfulness practices like slow breathing or brief moments of quiet reflection. Breaking down tasks into smaller, more manageable parts can make them less overwhelming. Establishing a consistent routine for these practices helps create a sense of stability. Remember that progress might be gradual, so let's be patient and kind to ourselves. Combining these straightforward strategies can contribute to regaining control over our attention and gradually lessening the impact of anxiety on our daily lives.

One way you can practice attention control is by asking safety questions. In my book *Face Off with Your Feelings*, I discuss that when we are conscious of our thoughts, they are most pliable because we are aware and can choose what to think. Putting this into practice can be as simple as asking ourselves questions or having someone else ask these "safety" questions. For example, if we were to say no to going to an event for work or family dinner, would that situation hurt us? Could that person hurt us? Not truly. Do we have to follow everyone else's way? No, we are adults and can make our own decisions. If we had to walk away from the person we feel hurt by, would we be okay? Yes. In fact, we may recognize the healing that will come from forgiveness through the Lord. Using this tool gives us the ability to ask ourselves questions in the situation to come to a more balanced understanding of our thoughts and the situation and produces a sense of safety. (Again, I recognize this is not dealing with situations where there are perceived physical threats in the present.) It allows us to be present to the Holy Spirit and consciously choose Him.

The second technique for stress and anxiety is to use our senses to practice awareness to keep us present. One way we can do this is by naming five things: five items we see around us, four things we can touch, three things we can hear, two things we can smell, and one thing we can taste. This doubles as a gratitude and praising exercise with the Lord thanking Him for his blessings and all that we can see, touch, hear, smell, and taste. As people made in His image, we always want to turn to the Father because we can do nothing apart from him. Practicing this connection with the Lord and practicing awareness of the present helps us stay connected to our reality and do it in a way we are grounding with the Lord.

Another way to keep us aware and in the present is to say everything we are aware of around us. For example, I am aware I have mud on my shoes. I am aware I am hungry. I am aware I am sad. This helps bring us back to the present and find relief. We do not live carnally, meaning through our senses, but we do get to acknowledge the goodness of God with them.

The last technique to help with stress and anxiety is learning to contain our anxiety and the emotions that come with it in a healthy way. This is called containment. For example, closing our journal after being honest with God about our feelings is a symbolic act of containment. Once we close the journal, we leave the distressing emotions, memories, sensations, and thoughts there. We know they are safe there. This isn't the same as ignoring our feelings, but it gives us a method to process intense or overwhelming emotions. However, little by little, we can take them out of containment and process them with the Lord, a coach, or a counselor.

Another example of containing is visualizing, using our powerful imaginations by giving each individual feeling over to God. Try it: I want you to close your eyes for this and picture yourself and Jesus with you, with his hand outstretched, taking every feeling from you. Let your feelings come before the Lord. It's where they are safe, secure, and seen. Give God everything that is causing you to feel wound up, worried, or stressed. Once you have handed everything over to God, sit with Him in His presence, find your breath, and open your eyes.

These are just a few ways you can begin to help your anxious feelings when they arise. I also wanted to share a few other ways I help my coaching clients manage anxiety.

Other Practical Ways to Help with Anxiety:

Reduce Caffeine Intake: Caffeine is a stimulant that can increase heart rate and contribute to feelings of restlessness and nervousness. Cutting back on caffeine can help regulate your energy levels and reduce symptoms of anxiety.

Move Your Body Every Day: Physical activity has been linked to the release of endorphins, the body's natural mood lifters. Regular exercise can also improve sleep quality, reduce stress hormones, and enhance overall well-being, providing a natural way to manage anxiety.

Ensure Adequate Caloric Intake: Proper nutrition is essential for maintaining physical and mental health. Inadequate calorie intake can lead to imbalances in neurotransmitters and energy levels, potentially exacerbating anxiety symptoms. Eating a balanced diet ensures your body receives the nutrients it needs to function optimally.

Consult a Healthcare Professional: Anxiety can have various underlying causes, including hormonal imbalances, nutritional deficiencies, or other medical conditions. Consulting with a doctor and undergoing thorough bloodwork can help identify any physiological factors contributing to anxiety. This holistic approach allows for a comprehensive understanding of your health, addressing potential root causes.

Seek Guidance from a Nutritionist: A nutritionist can provide personalized dietary advice, ensuring that you're fueling your body with the right nutrients. Certain foods can impact mood and energy levels, and a nutritionist can help create a balanced meal plan that supports mental health and reduces anxiety.

Consider Mental Health Professionals:
Anxiety often involves complex emotional and psychological factors. Seeking support from mental health professionals, such as therapists or counselors, can provide tools and coping strategies to manage anxiety effectively. They can offer a safe space to explore underlying issues and develop tailored strategies for long-term well-being.

Taking a holistic approach to anxiety management involves addressing physical, nutritional, and mental aspects. Consulting healthcare professionals, including doctors, nutritionists, and mental health professionals, ensures a comprehensive understanding of individual needs, leading to more effective and sustainable anxiety management strategies.

Talking About It
How we process and talk about the anxiety and stress we feel matters. We can not change our hearts by fixing our bodies. We can not change our bodies by hating our bodies. We simply can not change what we hate or continue to speak evil of. I know how frustrating it can be to feel like our bodies are against us. If we constantly speak about how stressed we are, how nothing will ever change, or if we just have to live this way, then we will get what we speak because we will live what we believe. Our bodies move in the direction of our most dominant thoughts. Not only our thoughts but also our deeper belief system have to be transformed.

Our words have power, so as we strive to let go of anxiety (the divided mind) and bring our mind back into a state of wholeness, consider these scriptures. Proverbs 12:6 describes what our words can do, "Our words have the power to destroy and the power to build up." The writer of Proverbs 18:21 tells us, "The tongue has the power of life and death, and those who love it will eat its fruit." Psalm 34:13 reminds us, "Keep your tongue from evil and your lips from speaking deceit." Proverbs 16:24 shares the impacts of our words, "Gracious words are like a honeycomb sweetness to the soul and health to the body." This challenges and convicts us to think about what we think and how we speak.

Our prayer for anxiety goes beyond anxiety being taken away. It's asking why it's there in the first place. To be kind and speak kindly of our bodies is not self-glorifying. It's reliance on the One who created our bodies and called them good. We know how easy it is for us to compare our bodies, wish our bodies were different, and hate our bodies. Colossians 3:12 says to clothe ourselves, *"Since God chose you to be the holy people he loves, you must clothe yourselves with tenderhearted mercy, kindness, humility, gentleness, and patience."* This is not just a command to fuel actions toward others; we can also embody these ourselves. Just like Jesus loved us first, and we respond in love to Him, as we live in communion with Him, we receive all of this from Him!

Closing Thoughts

I don't know the extent of your waiting or the anxiousness you may be suffering through, but I do know that God is faithful in the wilderness to lead us on the path to truth, restore our broken hearts, and redeem what felt stolen. Your prayers for anxiety are heard by God. We can rejoice in what is being awakened in us. Your healing journey from stress and anxiety isn't about praying away your emotions. Your body communicates specific needs, and checking in with them is good. Remember, through it all, Immanuel is His name; He is with you.

RESOURCES

Boundaries by Henry Cloud and John Townsend

Deadly Emotions by Don Colbert

A Still and Quiet Mind by Esther Smith

Try Softer by Aundi Kolber

You Are What You Love by James Smith

Holmes-Rahe Stress Inventory-take this self-evaluation to gain insight into your personal stress levels and experience. https://www.stress.org/holmes-rahe-stress-inventory

A Prayer for Anxiety

As we close out our time together and reflect on what God has shown us through this study, pray this with me:

>Father, guide my words today. Show me in Your word how to speak kind, be patient, and learn how to let go of my burdens and take Your yoke upon me. It's not about me trying to do better. It's about You consuming more of my heart. Let the words that leave my lips match the love You have for me. No matter the season, may my heart stay upon You. Father, I know You care for me so much. I know You love and know me better than anyone. Yet, my heart still hurts, and anxiousness finds me. Remind me today, in the moments I forget, that healing isn't dependent on whether someone recognizes my pain or not. It's dependent on my dependence on You that You heal the brokenhearted and bind up my wounds. In Jesus' name, amen!

Notes:

Notes:

Notes:

Notes:

Printed in Great Britain
by Amazon